Hey, Wait a Minute!

Keep Smiling
Dee Logan

Dee Logan

LEGACY PUBLISHING

Studio One, 201 Monroe Ave., Maitland, Florida 32751

Published by:
LEGACY PUBLISHING SERVICES, INC.
Studio One, 201 Monroe Avenue
Maitland, Florida 32751
www.legacypublishing.org

Copyright © 2001 by Dee Logan
ISBN 0-9708395-1-0
Cover Design by Gabriel H. Vaughn
Original cover cartoon by Andy Davenport

For comments to the author, scheduling interviews or
speaking engagements:
deelogan@intellistar.net
Dee Logan
P.O. Box 300301
Fern Park, FL 32730

Printed in United States of America

Dedication

This book is dedicated to my husband,
Kit Logan,
who has never said "no" to any of my dreams, and
always made sure they all came true.

Special Thanks

For her untiring effort in helping with the tediousness of
editing, and for her computer skills, and for her "We can
do this" attitude, I thank my sister, Betty "GG" Grimes.

A Note for Readers

Many references are made in this book to nieces and
nephews instead of daughters and sons. We have no
children, but feel as if we share our two nieces, Cheri and
Kay, and our nephew, Scott, with my sister,
Betty, and her husband, Jim.

HEY, WAIT A MINUTE!

This is a book of "stopping points" on the path of life.

It puts into words those things that either worry us, take us aback, or things at which we are totally aghast, especially the aging process.

Mentioned in the book is the revelation that life seems to come in decades rather than years to people approaching "seniorhood."

Read it from cover to cover, or let it put you to sleep at night by reading only one or two pages.

Hopefully, these humorous pages have a little "sting" of truth and yet a comforting poignancy in them.

Many of the situations are exaggerated for effect, and many exist only in my mind, but my perception of life is what this book is about.

Dee Logan

TABLE OF CONTENTS

CHAPTER 1   "Paranoia Pouting"

CHAPTER 2   "Shocking Revelations"

CHAPTER 3   "Husbandisms"

CHAPTER 4   "Personal Setbacks"

Chapter 5 "World at Large"

CHAPTER 6 "Miscellaneous Madness"

Hey, Wait a Minute!

CHAPTER

Paranoia Pouting

MY FIRST SOCIAL SECURITY CHECK
DESERVES FRAMING, BUT I THINK I'LL
RESIST THAT TEMPTATION AND PAY
THE PHARMACY.

Hey, Wait a Minute!

Why are they offering me Social Security? I'm only 62.

Our Government has some nerve!

Doesn't the Social Security Administration know that I'm still young?

I received a letter in yesterday's mail wanting to know if I planned to start receiving benefits on my next birthday when I'll turn 62.

That's five months away. The world could come to its end or I could win the lottery. Wish I would win the lottery - I'd tell them what they could do with their letter!

Don't get me wrong. Of course I want them to start sending me money. I'll use it for frivolous things, like trying to buy health insurance at my age, which is about as possible as having a turnip talk. Or maybe I'll use it for my prescriptions (wish it would cover them). At any rate, because I live in America, and have contributed during my work years, I am entitled to Social Security.

Just don't remind me 5 months before I turn 62!

Our Aunt loved to remind us that "Old age is not for sissies," and I thought at the time that she was just being funny. She died at age 94, and with each year she lived, that was her admonition.

Aunt Margaret, you were right.

Americans are a privileged society compared to most of the rest of the world because we do have help in our senior years.

I'm glad I live here, and I will be happy to have that first check arrive in my mailbox.

It deserves framing, but I think I'll resist that temptation and pay the pharmacy.

Hey, Wait a Minute!

Why do banks and government offices intimidate me? I always feel as if I've done something wrong.

If there is a phobia for "feeling guilty in public buildings" I have that malady. I am as guilt ridden in those buildings as I was to my mother's wagging index finger. Entering banks or government buildings is like entering a truth chamber where everyone there knows everything about your life from birth until today.

I wrote a bad check in 1961 when I was 21 to a convenience store called "Pot O Gold" in Atlanta. It was for $18. I was two days away from payday, and thought the deposit would beat the check to the bank. It didn't. I still apologize for that each time I stand in front of a bank teller. They look at me strangely when I say "Hello, sorry about the 'Pot O Gold' thing." They conduct my business, and whisper to each other as I'm leaving.

Government buildings are not quite so bad - unless the IRS is housed there. When I go for income tax forms, I feel as if a bevy of IRS agents are going to approach me, rub their hands together and scream "TIME FOR AN AUDIT!" I'm so careful about paying income tax that an audit would probably reveal that the government owed me money, but I still feel guilty and run out of the building after I get the forms.

I try to keep my banking and form hunting to a bare minimum. I know how silly it is to feel this way, but I do.

It's hard to get over that wagging index finger!

Hey, Wait a Minute!

Canned biscuits scare me to death!

To most people, it's a "pop." To me it's an "explosion!" It brings back childhood memories of squeezing a balloon and waiting for the bang when it finally would break. I could never stand that. Consequently, my husband has to open the canned biscuits in this house. You never know when to expect the "pop" or "explosion." Some sound off when you peel the paper, some when they are just laying in your hand, and worse are the one you have to rap on the counter. I'm a nervous wreck waiting for that sound!

I had rather watch the shower scene from "Psycho" than wait for that explosion.

I have a friend who has used canned biscuits since the day she married 40 years ago. But she's a biscuit sneak. The first thing she does is get the canister of loose flour and throw some on the counter, some on her blouse and a smear on her nose. She even coats her rolling pin. Then she takes the biscuits into the garage for the "pop" or "explosion." When she calls her husband to dinner, he sees her rolling pin, messed up nose, floured kitchen counter - even some on her blouse and brags to everyone that his wife always makes homemade biscuits, and has since they the day they were married.

Dishonest you say - ingenious, I say.

I could never do that though - not because I'm so honest, but because my husband has to open the biscuits.

They scare me to death!

"I ALWAYS FEEL AS IF MY ROUTE IS
FINISHED AFTER I DELIVER YOUR
MAIL. THE OTHER PART OF MY ROUTE
IS SO SIMPLE - AND LIGHT!"

Hey, Wait a Minute!

Why does my mailman hate me from July through December every year?

I can begin to read the little frown on his face about June 15th. He knows that in a couple of weeks, I will be receiving the first - CHRISTMAS CATALOGS! Yes, the catalog companies do begin their mailings on July 1st for Christmas. Unless you have opened your front door to a frowning mailman holding a plastic mail tub full of catalogs you haven't experienced the look of postal fatigue.

I make certain that I have soda or lemonade all year for this postman, and we chat and become friends from January through June. But it doesn't matter. He stops accepting favors July 1st, and makes statements like, "I always feel as if my route is finished after I deliver your mail, the other part of my route is so simple - and light." Or, "Would you like for me to bring you some forms to send to these companies to stop this junk mail?" I just tell him that I've tried to stop the catalogs and nothing works, and he doesn't believe me any more than he did last year when I told him the same thing.

One person's "junk mail" is another person's enjoyment. I love the catalogs. They provide hours of enjoyment to me and I even order sometimes, which puts a box on top of the catalogs in the plastic mail tub, and makes for a much sterner face on the mailman.

Several of my mailmen have transferred to another route throughout the 25 years I have been at this address. I don't know if my catalogs have caused the transfers, but if I had to guess I'd say maybe. This mailman seems to want to "stick it out" on my route, probably just to see if he can convert me to a normal postal customer.

We all have our battles!

Hey, Wait a Minute!

Why did I lie to the salesgirl at the mall about how many miles I had to drive to get to this store?

I wanted revenge!

I had done my job - my little arthritic fingers "did the walking" through the yellow pages and this very salesgirl answered the telephone and assured me that the shoes I inquired about were there - in my size - in my color - awaiting my arrival. I drove to the mall (2 miles), ran into the store with an outstretched arm holding my credit card and almost sang "I want my shoes."

"What kind of shoes would you like?" said the girl.

"The shoes I just called about less than 20 minutes ago," I said, and went on to give her the details. She disappeared into the back shoe room. She reappeared.

You guessed it.

"I'm sorry, but we don't have those in stock," she said smiling.

That's when I lied.

"Young lady, do you know that I drove 25 miles to get to this store because you assured me that you had these shoes? You have wasted my time, my gas, wear and tear on my car, my nerves and mostly my temper!"

Casually flipping her hair, she said, "I thought we had them, we have every other size."

But what she meant was, "Hey get over it Grandma, those shoes are ugly and out of style anyway. Why do you think they are on sale?"

While storming out of the store, I found the cutest sandals.

But, I made sure she didn't get credit for the sale.

Hey, Wait a Minute!

I started this needlepoint project 35 years ago - and it's only half finished!

At the rate my little flying fingers are going, I must live to the age of 97 to get closure on this project, and that's only if I keep up the lightning pace I've started.

I had visions of the beautiful covered bridge over running water hanging in the dining room in our first house when I purchased the canvas 35 years ago.

In our second house I thought it might add something wonderful to the décor in the den.

By the time we moved into our third house, I had relegated it to the laundry room thinking it might add a note of warmth as I was folding clothes.

Our tastes have changed from "country" to "modern" and it is hard to find a proper place in a modern décor for a needlepoint covered bridge with running water beneath - done in 1960's golds, browns, and oranges.

I plan to finish the project. I plan to have it framed. We have no plans for buying another house, but, I have found an empty space just above my husband's table saw in the garage that could probably use a beautiful covered bridge with water running beneath.

So the $14.99 original investment (including yarn) will have provided years and years of pleasure in the craft and a beautiful picture to add warmth to our garage.

My fingers will fly like the wind!

WHY AM I HAVING
"SENIOR MOMENTS"? I THINK
I'M JUST NOT CONCENTRATING.

Hey, Wait a Minute!

Why am I having "senior moments?" I think I'm just not concentrating.

Have you ever been surprised at a club meeting when your name is announced as hostess for next week's meeting?

Not only had you forgotten that there was a meeting next week, but you certainly did not remember being asked to be hostess.

I don't know what happens to our brain cells. I think they are smart enough to only regenerate the very necessary ones, and let the others die a natural death. It may not be our brain cells at all, but most probably our memory.

Memory requires concentration, and I have found that harder to do within the past few years.

I have introduced an acquaintance to my husband using the wrong name, and I have introduced a close friend and club member, Barbara Hunt, as Barbara Bush to my entire garden club.

Luckily Barbara has a wonderful sense of humor and her first statement to the club was "The President sends his greetings."

I'll always love her for that, as it was a wonderful and forgiving "ice breaker," and it set a happy tone for the rest of the meeting..

I think we volunteer too much, do too much, run our lives in a panic mode and then wonder why we can't remember an acquaintance's name or introduce someone using the wrong name.

I plan to use the brain cells that I have left for the important things from now on..

There are only a few of those and a monstrous amount of unimportant ones.

Hey, Wait a Minute!

Women don't snore!

My mother said that women's throats were different than men's, and it was therefore impossible for women to snore - especially Southern "ladylike" women.

I believe her.

My husband does not believe her!

He describes my sleep as something akin to two chain saws - one being fired up as I inhale, and the other being fired up as I exhale.

He is prone to exaggeration.

I have explained to him countless times that women don't have Adam's apples and our throats are built differently, and it's probably Caledonia, our cat, that he is hearing, but he is not buying it. He's not buying it to the extent that he has given me a nickname - "Poulan."

It is embarrassing to me for him to come into the bedroom with cotton balls stuffed into his ears. For years, I just thought he had an ear condition. That condition worsened as I got older and heavier, and now he wears aircraft worthy ear plugs to bed.

As I said, he is prone to exaggeration.

I still am not convinced that I snore, but on a trip with the girls to a state convention, several of my roommates and I stayed awake all night just in case. Allowing your husband hear you "not snore" is one thing, but you certainly don't want to take a chance that your girlfriends will hear you "not snore."

One of my roommates said her husband called her "Black and Decker."

She didn't explain why.

Hey, Wait a Minute!

Of course I wear "women's sizes" in clothes, but it's because the others won't fit!

Size 14w to 24w, sometimes referred to as 14 wide to 24 wide, or if you prefer, X large to XXXXX large.

Yes I am in that group of what advertising agencies call "Big and Beautiful," or my favorite, "Big Momma." I have added dimensions.

This makes me a big person, not a bad person.

Most stores hide this clothing in an entirely different department from the "regular" sizes. The "Women's Sizes" can be seen after you walk through "Small Appliances," "Domestics," and "Table Linens" so that it will in no way detract from the size 4's through size 16's.

In most stores, our department is on an entirely different floor from the others - up there with lingerie on the second or third floor.

I guess the management must feel that if we have to search it out, we'll just go away and there will soon be no need to stock "those" sizes.

I can think of no other motivation.

The designers are finally working with us though and have improved the styles during the past few years and for that we are most appreciative.

I do wish they had this double-knit bikini in orange though. The lime green makes me look fat!

Don't say it!

Hey, Wait a Minute!

Why did I think it was a good idea to buy a walker at a garage sale?

Ok, I love machinery and industrial design I kept telling myself, and this walker folded up with a touch of a big fat lever that felt nice on the hands.

It required practically no storage space - or more to the point - hiding space. I would never want anyone to know that I had purchased such a shrine to the aged.

Yesterday, the day of the purchase, I had my usual touch of arthritis in my knees and hips and shoulders and fingers when I saw the walker and frankly, fantasized about using it to walk back to the car. But, I told the lady who sold it to me for $20 that I was buying it for my grandmother.

Then I began to have buyer's remorse and decided I would put it in my next garage sale. We "mature" ladies do just that - buy from one garage sale, pay to have a storage place and then have our own garage sale so we can lose about double the amount we paid for the item originally.

So it was settled - I bought it for my next garage sale. That's what I would tell my husband and anyone else that asked. I won't need to admit to anything except being enterprising.

I think I might forget where I put it the next time I have a garage sale though. There's a comfort of a kind knowing that it is hidden away under my bed and can be reached with little effort.

If I ever do get old, and need a walker, well at least I'm prepared.

I just hope none of my old college chums read this!

Hey, Wait a Minute!

Why do they always seat me at the table nearest the kitchen - or the restroom?

I have wonderful manners, I don't wave my fork around when I'm talking, or chew with my mouth open, or get loud or boisterous during the meal. I don't tuck my napkin into my collar, slurp soup, wear a baseball cap while dining or do anything that would offend other diners.

So, why does the hostess at any restaurant take one look at me and decide that the lady for the back table is here? Maybe it's because I look placid and they think I won't ask for another table, or maybe they try to give that table as a first shot to anyone who comes in the building.

It's a hard table to fill, because if you have ever had it, you know you are either dodging kitchen trays or watching guys check their zipper on the way out. When the door opens to the restroom an unappetizing flash of toilets and aroma confronts this table.

To quote an unhappy diner, "I'm mad as hell and I'm not going to take it anymore."

That decision made, I went for lunch today, and the "favorite" table was available, and I refused it - good for me!

I did, however, wait an additional 20 minutes for another table and had to acquiesce, and accept one in the "smoking section."

After 5 minutes of inhaling smoke from my fellow diners/smokers, I was longing for my table by the kitchen or restroom.

I don't know who gets the normal non-smoking tables, but I plan to have a "fiver" handy the next time I do lunch.

Hey, Wait a Minute!

CHAPTER 3

Shocking Revelations

Hey, Wait a Minute!

When did my duties as President of my garden club take precedence over a weekend at the beach?

We had planned a retreat to the beach for weeks. I was looking forward to the relaxation and "toes in the water playing with the sand" kind of mini vacation. Reading a cheap, tawdry novel would be the only exercise my brain would get all weekend. Getting out of bed at noon was an option, and falling asleep at 3am was an option. At the beach there are no schedules and no stress. I was ready!

Reality kicked in about two days before our departure.

My ego had won a battle over my good sense about five months ago and I had agreed to accept the presidency of my garden club. Not a big deal you say? This garden club is like no other garden club. Some of the 75 members are young, and some are seniors, but no matter what their age happens to be physically, they are all age 25 mentally and actively. When they commit to a project - they commit to a project! Nothing is done haphazardly. Everything is done perfectly and with aplomb. Their (our) flower show was the same weekend as my ill-fated beach retreat.

The flower show could have gone perfectly without me, as I was a very small part of it. However, as the day neared, it became more exciting than the beach, and I could not imagine how the show could possibly occur without my being there. Talk about ego! My loyalty shifted from myself to a wonderful group of ladies and I felt not a twinge of regret.

The show was perfect, as I knew it would be, and after we cleaned up the hall I came home to a hot bubble bath, laid back, started reading my cheap tawdry novel and my toes went into the water and played with the sand - uh - bubbles.

Hey, Wait a Minute!

Who invited all these old people to my 40th class reunion?

The older we get the more our eyes disguise. Our eyes see us differently than other people do. This is a blessing, as our eyes seem to remember the best parts of us and overlook the rest.

After losing my breakfast and my composure the morning I received an invitation to my 40th college reunion I decided to recharge, adjust my attitude and my expectations, and attend this event. It would be great to renew old acquaintances and catch up on all the news. I would show all my classmates that I was different - I didn't look 40 years older. (Refer to the first sentence.)

I returned my "I will attend" postcard, and realized that I had only two weeks to lose 38 pounds, find a designer dress, get my hair styled and have a make-up makeover.

My eyes failed to deceive me at the reunion because I looked just like everyone else. Some were still thin and some were heavier, but all older than I had expected. Some I remembered and some, not. The sad part was that some were gone, but there was a golden thread of friendship that ran throughout the class. For this, I am thankful. It was great seeing all the photographs of everyone's children and of their grandchildren. I happily showed photos of my "grand" nieces and nephews.

In 10 years I am sure that I will receive another invitation to my 50th college reunion, and I am just as sure that I will lose my breakfast, and my composure at the idea.

I am also just as sure that it will conflict with that two-week trip to Europe that I've been planning for 10 years.

I'll remember my classmates with a toast in Paris or Rome.

Hey, Wait a Minute!

When did I start longing for bed at 9:30? I used to party all night!

I have found that all cats thrive on a schedule. Their little internal clocks chime at every mealtime and every treat-time. Each day, you can rely on them to use the litter box at the same time.

I am not a cat.

I must find a way to convince my body and mind that I am too young for "getting up" and "going to bed" schedules.

At exactly 9:30 every night for the last couple of years, my chime has gone off. My entire body screams that it has had all of this day it plans to take and will now shut down until I have given it some rest and sleep. Wham! - bath - bed!

Hey, wait a minute! 9:30 was the time we used to meet for dinner when we were in the Jaycees. I used to get more accomplished after 9:30 p.m. than the Army does all morning long. (You've seen the commercial).

Also, I wake up, and get up at 6:00 a.m. There's none of this lovely lounging around in bed anymore. If I lounge, I get a headache.

It has been said that a repetition of 13 times makes anything a habit. I have a habit!

My cats love it, they think I've come over to their side and am now one of them.

I think I can handle that.

OK, I'VE FINALLY FACED IT.
I'M A 62 YEAR OLD FAT BLOND,
BUT VERY LOVABLE, AND A DYNAMO!

Hey, Wait a Minute!

I've finally accepted it, I'm a fat blond. But I'm lovable, and I'm a dynamo!

Understand I use the term blond very loosely. Underneath this boxed platinum color, I'm probably as gray as the morning fog in London. I say probably, because I've never checked, and don't intend to for awhile. I have noticed that my hairdresser only uses toner instead of bleach plus toner, which means that she doesn't need to "whiten" my hair before she tones (colors) it. That should give me a clue.

I'm ignoring that clue.

I also choose to ignore the 30+ pounds that have mysteriously appeared on my body during the past few years. This is "happy fat" and doesn't count except on scales and in dress sizes. All the mirrors in my house show only from the neck up, and I still live in that world where ignorance is bliss, and if I can't see it, it's not there. As long as I can believe that theory, I'm sticking to it.

I think people make too much out of the way other people look and don't bother to see the way they act or feel about themselves and others or the way they feel about life .

I suppose that's just human nature. But "fat, blond, lovable and dynamo" don't really matter as long as you are happy with yourself and your world in general is serene.

About the "dynamo" part of this title - I only said that to make me feel good. Truthfully, I'm pretty laid back.

But hey, I can have goals!

Hey, Wait a Minute!

My preference in periodicals has changed from "National Enquirer" to "National Gardener."

I don't care how naughty Whitney's husband is or how naked Jennifer gets while sunbathing or how undeserved the fortune is from Anna's 90-year-old dead husband. I simply don't care.

I do care that my roses have bugs, and that my azaleas have killer vines growing in them and that my geraniums are fading from red to pink.

I don't know when this happened.

Curling up with the juicy gossip from celebrities, even though in my heart I knew 99% of it was untrue, was a favorite pastime.

I think, however, that many things start to reverse when you reach a certain age.

On an episode of my favorite sitcom, "Golden Girls," Sophia laments that when you get old it seems as if something is always being taken away from you - your hearing, your eyesight, and other things.

I think there is something given to you as you age, and that is the wisdom to choose what is important in life. This doesn't mean you lose your zest for life, but that your circle of caring shrinks only to include the important stuff.

Having a few wrinkles, a few aches and pains, and being a little forgetful are tiny prices to pay for contentment.

Life and love both improve with age.

I think someone planned it that way!

Hey, Wait a Minute!

When did late night phone calls start being a worry instead of a joy?

The later the better!

Of course it doesn't matter if I'm sleeping. All I have to do is just turn over and go back to sleep.

Call anytime - it's always great to hear from you.

Those phrases are reserved for the young.

Everything changes!

"The later the better" becomes "Call after 10pm, only if you have a death wish"

"Of course it doesn't matter if I'm sleeping" becomes "If that stupid telephone awakens me after 10pm, I'm up for the night, Tylenol and hot chocolate notwithstanding!"

"All I have to do is turn over and go back to sleep" becomes "All I have to do is turn over and go back to sleep - TOMORROW NIGHT! - IF I'M LUCKY."

"Call anytime" becomes "I have a 10 to 10 rule. No calls before 10am, and no calls after 10pm."

"It's always great to hear from you" becomes "It's always great to hear from you - after 10am and before 10pm."

Only emergency calls should ring the phone after 10pm. That should be a rule enforced by a "Telephone Police." If I receive a phone call after 10pm I want to wake up frightened because, according to my rules, something is wrong.

The young can have their midnight conversations and those wonderful "love calls" from their sweeties. They are important and a wonderful part of growing up. I too was a telephone junkie, but, I've been there, done that, would not wear the tee shirt if I had one.

Now I need sleep - beautiful sleeeezzzzzzzzzzz.

CAN ANYBODY OUT THERE HELP ME BUY
SOME TIRES?

Hey, Wait a Minute!

I can't buy tires anymore.
I need to go to tire college!

It is far easier to buy a new car than to replace the tires on your old one. My parents used to make a joke about keeping a new car until the ashtrays were full and then they would trade it in.

It's not a joke anymore. When it's time to replace the tires on a car, you have two choices. Either throw up your hands and accept what the tire salesman is telling you - or trade the car. There are so many numbers and symbols and combinations of numbers and symbols on the side of a new tire that you would need a textbook just to figure them out.

I went tire shopping, and asked for "round black ones" and the salesman very politely said, "Well, that's a start" and began rolling numbers off his tongue sounding like a computer that stutters. I nodded "yes" or "no" for awhile to his questions and finally ran out of the store and headed for the nearest car lot.

I think a huge selling point for new cars would be if they came equipped with 2 sets of tires. Even if you had to pay to store the extra set it would be worth it.

I don't think the average person is knowledgeable enough to conduct his own life anymore with all the new compounds and materials and medicines that have been discovered.

Maybe a new career path will be "Life Conductor" in the near future. The degree would take years to earn.

In the meantime, can anybody out there help me buy some tires?

Hey, Wait a Minute!

I've started keeping TUMS by my bedside!

I will give up my Tabasco sauce when they pry it from my cold dead hands!

Kicking and screaming, I have lessened my consumption of jalapenos and extra-hot garlic chicken wings.

I said lessened - not ceased.

When I was a child in South Georgia, my daddy kept us supplied with those little hot peppers that measure thousands on the Scoville unit chart. He loved them and I loved him, so I developed a taste for "hot" as an addition to any food.

I have read articles that say these little peppers sooth one's endorphins and make them feel wonderful. When my endorphins feel wonderful so do I.

Here's my problem.

Last night, after a great Mexican dinner that left my mouth numb, I found myself automatically reaching for the bottle on my bedside table.

To my horror, it was antacid - Tums.

When did my stomach decide that I couldn't handle Mexican anymore? Moreover, when did I feel it necessary to buy - Tums?

I lied to myself and said I bought them because it was a great way to get calcium, but deep down where no one lives but me, I knew it was to soothe the hot away so that I could sleep.

And I did sleep - just after the warm milk.

It calmed down my raging endorphins.

Hey, Wait a Minute!

Why am I embarrassed, to admit that I enjoy watching TV?

The dumber the sitcom the better!

Being a "couch potato" or more truthfully a "Lazyboy potato" is a beautiful part of my daily routine. Staring at the television, and getting into a sitcom that brings laughter and sometimes tears or groans is a place I enjoy - yes, sports people - enjoy! I appreciate the decades of development and the millions of dollars that someone spent to bring this bit of joy into my life. The acting and writing may need help, but the efforts are superb.

Thank you, whoever invented the remote control, and thank you, whoever invented the cable and satellite dishes that bring 340 channels for me to surf through without moving from my Lazyboy recliner.

There are many things on TV that cause my little remote control to literally fly by without a second look, and there are many things that teach me stuff that I would never know, or care to know, including some of the sex and nature channels.

I love to watch the most boring channel on television - The Weather Channel - and can stay tuned to it for hours.

The sports are great, and the news informative, but the movies and sitcoms are unsurpassed.

I have got to get a life!

Hey, Wait a Minute!

When did my knees get too arthritic to climb into an SUV and my butt get too wide to sit in a sports car?

A van is all that is left for me.

Luckily, I love vans - so much so that I'm enjoying my third one right now.

I hate to admit why I love vans, but between you and me, isn't it wonderful just to turn your back to the seat and sit down? There's no climbing into a tall seat that is 5 feet off the ground and no falling on your keister into a seat that is a foot and a half off the ground. Just sit down and screw your bottom around until your little feet are touching the pedals.

Heaven!

Vans are also nice for hauling things like grandchildren, plants and flowers, groceries and antiques - and knees and keisters.

I think vans are made for the "extremely mature."

I know there are those who would argue for the SUV, however, the only trail I plan to blaze is a trip over the speed bumps on the way to the grocery store, and that does not call for 4-wheel drive - an option on most SUV's.

We have owned many sports cars in our married life, and even raced some of them, but that was when all of our body parts were young and eager for speed and style.

I think we either get smarter or stodgier about such things as we age, but I prefer to think more caring.

At least about our knees and keisters.

WHY DOES MY PURSE WEIGH 24 LBS.
IS MY CAT IN THERE?

Hey, Wait a Minute!

Why does my purse weigh 24 pounds? Is my cat in there?

I know when I need medication to sleep because of an aching right arm, that it's time to clean out my purse.

The following morning, I clear off the guest bed and turn my purse upside down. The bed is only "queen size" and therefore not big enough to hold all that comes tumbling out. 8 shades of lipstick at my age is a little excessive. Also, I have a habit of throwing change in the bottom of the purse, which can add 1 ½ to 2 lbs. in "purse weight."

Listed below are the contents of my purse:

Wallet with 16 credit cards, drivers license and very little money, telephone, "wizard" organizer, 8 shades of lipstick, eye shadow, eye pencil, blush, checkbook, 4 ball point pens, camera, 2 extra rolls of film, full size hairbrush, comb, nail polish, nail file, nail clippers, scissors, knife, address book, plastic lottery envelope (with tickets), business card case with no cards inside, 6 envelopes of "Shout" stain remover, bottle of hand cream, small can of hairspray, 30 cough drops, small bottle of Tylenol, 8 wadded up receipts from purchases, $14 worth of quarters nickels and dimes, 46 pennies, 3 small screwdrivers and a wrench.

Listed below are things I need in my purse:

Wallet, telephone, checkbook, 1 lipstick—and maybe the wrench.

I suppose my stint in Girl Scouts taught me to "Be Prepared," but the older I get the more medication I seem to need for my poor aching arm.

Hey, Wait a Minute!

CHAPTER 3

Husbandisms

WE'VE HAD A WONDERFUL 38 YEARS
TOGETHER, AND STILL WORK AT MAKING
OUR MARRIAGE GREAT. IT IS.

Hey, Wait a Minute!

When I woke up this morning, I had been married 38 years!

My husband can rest easy in the knowledge that there will be no illicit love affairs for me.

I have post-nasal drip and wear flannel night-gowns.

It's not a pretty sight. The worse times are going to bed at night, and getting up in the morning. Going to bed involves Mentholatum, Tylenol, and cotton balls (I won't go into detail), and getting up in the morning involves a wet hacking cough and screwed up hair that looks like two horns on top of my head.

It's far from sexy.

Heck, it's not even presentable!

Thankfully, these problems occurred slowly over the years, one at a time, which is the way they had to be accepted by me and by my husband. Neither of us could have handled them any other way.

Thank goodness love is deaf and blind.

We've had a wonderful 38 years together, and still work at making our marriage great. It is.

Even without the post-nasal drip and hacking cough, and head horns, I don't think he would have anything to worry about.

Illicit love affairs require so much energy and deception.

My mind is too old to think up lies.

Hey, Wait a Minute!

Never say to a headwaiter,
"Why don't you select the wine"
- unless you bear a striking resemblance
to his mother!

The cry of "OW" was heard by our traveling companions as well as by the entire dining car. It came from my husband whose shin had been the recipient of a kick from my pointed-toe pump.

We were on the Orient Express having a luxurious dinner, and living a dream that we had saved for years to have.

When asked to select a dinner wine, he had very sweetly said to the waiter "Why don't you select the wine?"

That's when the kick came. I could imagine our Visa card being maxed out by a $400 bottle of wine that we would be obligated to buy.

The waiter smiled and disappeared and the dining-car diners seemed to enjoy our embarrassment with their "titters."

We were as vulnerable as we would have been had we come to dinner naked.

I misjudged my trusting husband and his assessment of waiters, and I misjudged the waiter who appeared with a beautiful and tasty bottle of wine saying it was his personal favorite. We enjoyed it tremendously - and the $35 was well within our means. When we returned to our stateroom for the night, I apologized once more for the kick and for the doubts I had about the waiter.

Secretly though, I still think we were lucky, and I think that I must have reminded the waiter of his mother.

I'm really sorry about that big bruise on my husband's shin - it lasted a really long time.

Hey, Wait a Minute!

Fred, Dave, Mike, Charlie and Bruce are all great friends of my husband!

When my husband named his hammer "Mike," I thought it was cute because of the detective series. However, when I was helping him hang a picture the other day and he asked if I would go into the garage and bring "Fred" to him I started to worry.

"Who's Fred?" I asked.

"You know, the small punch" he said.

"Why did you name the small punch "Fred?" I asked.

"It just looked like a 'Fred'" he replied.

This man is spending way too much time in his workshop with his tools.

"Do all of your tools have names?" I asked.

"Sure" he answered, "most of them are just named Dave or Bruce or Charlie - you know Dave drill, Bruce pliers, and Charlie clamps."

"And Fred punch?" I said.

"Yeah," he said, "Did you find Fred?" I handed him the punch.

At this point I began to wonder if he was "putting me on" and I began laughing like it was a gigantic joke.

"You really had me going," I said laughing.

"You don't laugh at a man's tools," he said seriously. "Fred, Dave, Mike, Charlie and Bruce have served me well and don't deserve to be laughed at."

On my way to the bedroom to make a phone call to his Doctor, I turned to look back at him. He was doubled over with laughter!

I picked up "Fred" and with great reserve, took it back to the garage instead of throwing it at him.

Hey, Wait a Minute!

**Parking places are not a problem to me.
My husband drops me off at the
front door of the store before he
starts looking for one.**

My sister, who lives in Atlanta, can close her eyes and decide which parking space she would like to have at any given store, drive there, and magically the space is vacant or vacated just as she arrives. I think "voodoo" is involved, but that's another story. She doesn't realize what a gift this is, and simply takes it for granted.

I, on the other hand, can drain my gas tank dry riding around any parking lot, searching for a space that doesn't require hiking boots and a backpack to get to the front door of the store.

A problem ceases to be a problem when a solution is found - enter my husband.

I've removed my hiking boots and backpack from the van and replaced them with him. He drives me to the front door and then if he's lucky, by the time I finish my shopping, he has found a parking space. We even have two-way radios so that I can tell him when my purchases and I are ready to be collected - again - at the front door.

So, even though I don't have the "gift" or practice the "voodoo" necessary to obtain parking spaces, I think my solution is just as good, or even better.

Besides, so far, my husband has read fourteen novels waiting for me to call him on the two-way.

EXITING THE TRAIN SHOW, THE MEN WERE
SMILING AS IF SANTA HAD JUST VISITED.
BUT THE WOMEN HAD A DAZED WIDE-EYED
LOOK AS IF THEY HAD BEEN ASKED A
QUESTION THEY COULDN'T ANSWER.

Hey, Wait a Minute!

I've got it straight now.
Flower shows are for women -
Train shows are for men.

Sitting in the lobby of a high school auditorium waiting for my husband to appear from a model train show, I began to watch the couples leave the show. The men were all smiling, as if Santa had just visited, but the majority of women had a dazed wide-eyed look as if they had just been asked a question they couldn't answer. Let's get down to the nitty-gritty - it was a look of boredom!

I kept watching and realized that I had seen this look before. Then I remembered! It was the exact look that men have when they emerge from a flower show.

It's nice to do things together, but I can assure you that the men in our lives don't even know we are with them when they are at a model train show, and would prefer that we not even speak. If the women are honest, I think they would prefer the same at a flower show.

The men know how many bolts and rivets it took to build a Conrail SD40-2 train engine in 1972, and we know how many flowers it takes to create the perfect Hogarth curve for a prize-winning floral design, and "ne'er the twain shall meet!"

That creates a kind of balance to marriage and life, which is pleasing, if you take the time to think about it.

I just can't imagine why they care about how many bolts and rivets it took for the 1972 engine.

Who's counting?

IT WAS A GREAT BUY, AND ONLY HAD
240,000 MILES ON IT.
AND IT WAS YELLOW!

Hey, Wait a Minute!

Why did my husband buy a 1983 Volvo station wagon with 240,000 miles on it?

"It's yellow," he said.

"It will make a wonderful second car for us" he said.

"Volvos last five times longer than other cars," he said.

"After I wax it, it will look brand new," he said.

When I didn't seem impressed by these virtues of the car he ended with, "It followed me home, can I keep it?"

"Did I mention that it was yellow?" he asked.

Then he made his first serious mistake.

"You can name it," he said.

To him, this car was "sunshine yellow." When I saw it sitting in the front driveway, it was a rather putrid shade of "carnival gold" - like strained squash that had been in a baby too long..

So I named it - "Vomit."

Were there a highway to the moon, "Vomit" could have traveled it's entire length - and part way back to earth. That's how many miles it showed on its speedometer. There was some rust, which he quickly repaired working 12 hours a day for a few weeks, and then he waxed it, making it look like shiny vomit. I don't know why men fall in love with cars and want to save them from sure "junkyard death," but they do. I think it's the same thing that makes women want to own 100 pairs of shoes.

So I accepted Vomit, caressed its little fenders, and one day, may even drive it to the store.

It makes a wonderful second car for us.

Did I mention it was yellow?

Hey, Wait a Minute!

Leave my dust bunnies and cobwebs alone. I'm saving them for Halloween decorations!

Before my husband retired a few years ago, he left for his office one morning and the moment he got there, my phone rang.

"Dear," he said, "in the northwest top corner of the living room is a cobweb."

Being "directionally challenged," I had no idea which corner was the northwest, and could not understand why he had not just swiped the cobweb down.

So, I quickly came back with "I'm saving it." I don't know why, it just came out of my mouth. Then I backed it up with "I hope you didn't destroy it."

There was silence at the other end of the phone for a long moment and then an incredulous "Why?"

"For Halloween," I said.

He followed with a meek "OK" and hung up the phone.

I don't know at what point during the day it dawned on him that he had been "had," but it evidently did. He arrived home with a look of a "cobweb warrior" on his face, got out of his car, went to the broom closet, got the broom and swiped the cobweb into oblivion.

I did not get taken out to dinner that night, but we both learned something from this experience.

He learned that his wife is nuts, and I learned which was the northwest corner of my living room.

If he ever finds a dust bunny under the bed, I plan to tell him it's a pet!

Hey, Wait a Minute!

What? Huh? Say Again? —

As we age, our hearing and sight diminish somewhat, but there are those who make an art of seeing and hearing only when they wish.

My friend thinks her husband has a condition that she has named Selective Hearing Impairment Tendency. She refers to this ailment by its first letters, which I won't print, as this is a family book.

Her annoyance at his question of "What did you say, Hon?" is made obvious with her answer because it is usually shouted at decibels that are off the scale. She is convinced that her husband can't hear just to frustrate her, and that he hears perfectly well when asked if he wants a martini, or if he cares to go to a movie. According to her, the things he has trouble hearing involve shopping, lawn mowing and trash removal.

I made a suggestion to her that she have his hearing tested at the local hearing center and she thought that to be a wonderful idea.

She went straight inside and asked her husband if he would consider going for the test and he answered in no uncertain terms with "What did you say, Hon?"

WE KNEW WE WERE IN TROUBLE WHEN THE
CLERK AT THE GARDEN STORE
AUTOMATICALLY PLACED A MACHETE ON
THE COUNTER WITH OUR OTHER
PURCHASES.

Hey, Wait a Minute!

When did gardening become a sport instead of a pastime?

I think it was the day we moved to Florida, and found that plastic would root and grow here with enough water, sunshine, and soil.

There is plenty of all of that in Florida.

First day here at the gardening supply store after buying a hoe, clippers, hedge trimmers and a mower, we knew we were in trouble when they had a sale on machetes, and the salesman automatically put one with our purchases.

"You'll need one of these a few weeks after planting" he said.

If you are not a homeowner in Florida, you marvel at the lush green vegetation and beautiful tropical blooms. If you are a homeowner, invest in the machete, and get the heaviest and sharpest one you can manage.

My husband and I were taking a stroll around our swimming pool last night. We were admiring the lovely hibiscus bushes (14 feet tall) and the beautiful ligustrum bush (20 feet tall) when we happened to notice that a 10-foot "volunteer" water oak tree had grown up in the center of the ligustrum. Now I admit that we don't take a nightly stroll around the pool, but I would swear that the water oak was not there last week.

We decided at that point that we had outgrown the machete and headed for Home Depot where, luckily, they were having a sale on chainsaws.

Whrrrrrrr! —— every man's dream.

I SUGGESTED TO MY HUSBAND THAT HE
TAKE YOGA TO BECOME MORE FLEXIBLE!

Hey, Wait a Minute!

I always have my husband's very best interests at heart, no matter how it turns out.

He'll never learn. He always takes my suggestions at face value. If I tell him it will be fun, or good for him, he accepts that and follows through with my suggestion.

I'm way low on percentages for things that worked, and way high on those that did not work, some of which caused him actual pain and suffering. My defense is that it was a good idea at the time. Not much of a defense, but it's all I have.

My suggestions have included ballroom dancing, jazzercise, weight lifting, jogging, YMCA floor exercises and yoga. There were others, but they were the ones that caused actual pain and I'm trying to forget them. I still think that if he had concentrated he could have mastered yoga, but that's a sore subject.

Yes, I meant the pun!

It took him three days (after he finally got untangled) to walk without a limp and his karma was very disturbed. I think it was a successful adventure as he learned what "karma" meant, but he thought the price was too high for that knowledge.

He has requested that my next ideas for him not involve body movement and suggested that I look into something like whittling, creating stained glass objects, or even "Rosie Greer" needlework.

I'll consider his thoughts, however I just read about a class that begins next week on rock climbing.

Those little outfits and shoes are really cute for rock climbing!

They would look great on him!

Hey, Wait a Minute!

What am I doing at a wrestling match? I thought "Dusty Rhodes" were the ones in the country that haven't been paved.

He's going to pay - and pay big.

I think there might be 10 or 12 antique shows in this for me.

I ignored my good sense, overcame my resistance, put on my happy face and agreed to accompany my husband to a wrestling match.

I sat next to a very boisterous and happy lady who was quite heavy and really needed two marked places on the bench to be comfortable. I was in her second marked off bench seat. Before the evening was over I felt as if I were one of the contestants, and that by all rights the 2-seat lady and I should be engaged.

It got that personal!

We shared disaster when her favorite lost his match, and joy when the one she hated lost his match. I was "high fived," punched, hugged and deafened by this loyal fan.

That is when I "upped the ante" to 100 antique shows.

Sitting next to me, and observing this "super fan," was my husband who had no choice but agreement. I never watched the ring where the wrestling occurred, and felt that the wrestlers should have been watching us. Our show was much better, and the action was real.

I will enjoy having an escort to my next 100 antique shows. We've already been to 18.

When we near the 100 mark, I just might agree to that "Tractor Pull" he wants to attend.

For a price!

Hey, Wait a Minute!

CHAPTER

Personal Setbacks

When did I start being careful instead of reckless? I used to be a wild thing!

I carry spot remover in my purse!

I do!

I have little foil envelopes of spot remover - 6 or 7 of them - neatly placed in the inside compartment of my purse. Not only do I carry them - I offer them to anyone with a spill on their clothing. I endure the looks that say "Who is this old biddy, and why does she care if I have a spot on my blouse?"

There are old things we do and there are young things. This "old" spot remover thing is akin to the "young" thing of spitting on a handkerchief and wiping the dirt off your child's face. And I know it is just as annoying. I don't know when I became "Mrs. Clean," and I'm sorry about it, but I just can't seem to help it.

It all started at a garden club function, when I met an "old biddy" who offered me a little foil envelope of spot remover when I spilled red punch on my white blouse, and she became my hero. I think it's nice to have an "old biddy" with spot remover as one's hero. It somehow elevates some of the more real life things to a higher status.

Sports figures seemed to have "dropped the ball" (sorry) when it comes to being heroes. Movie stars and politicians have sunk to very low levels in the hero category. So, I think I'll stick with my "old biddy" and her spot remover. After all, she saved a $40 blouse from extinction!

I can't think of anything that sports figures, movie stars, and politicians have done lately that's worth $40.

Hey, Wait a Minute!

Of course I take a steamy bubble bath every night - but only for medicinal purposes!

It's medicine for the soul!

When I exhaust my supply of bubble bath, I have been known to use dishwashing liquid, or in severe cases, laundry detergent. I don't recommend this however, as it has a tendency to turn your skin into a dry flaky sheet of scales.

I will take dry, flaky sheets of scales as long as it allows me to play "toe the bubble," "blow the bubble" or "throw the bubble"- 40 years of games I invented to help me enjoy this respite from the day. Not that the bubbles need any help, for they have games of their own.

They play with your mind, and help it relax and forget the tribulations of the day.

They also help you remember the triumphs of the day.

They tell you not to worry about the trials of the day.

These airy little foamies of nothing can stand up to - and defeat - anything you throw their way. They bestow a vacation from noise, problems, and hurry and worry, and you can enjoy this retreat as long as the drain is closed, and the bubbles remain. I have sculpted everything from "Venus de Milo" to "Gumby" using the bubbles as my clay.

Time wasted you say - never - It's time regained.

A few candles and some wine, and I just might invite a friend!

Hey, Wait a Minute!

When did I start using wooden clothespins to close potato chip bags?

It's such a stodgy, "fuddy-duddy" thing to do, and I hated when my grandmother did it when I was growing up. Why couldn't she just twist the top of the bag and hope for the best, or why didn't she just eat up the chips, or throw away the ones that were left? Instead, she would carefully fold the top of the bag down six or seven times and then clamp it shut with the wooden clothespin. It made me crazy.

There is a plastic covered wire frame can holder attached to the Inside of my pantry door, and when I opened it today there were 8 or 10 wooden clothespins clamped to one of the wire frame bottoms just waiting for my potato chips.

When did I turn into my grandmother?

I realized that I had been using those wooden clothespins for my potato chip bags for years. It just seemed the natural thing to do. The clothespins work, and the chips stay fresh, and I really don't mind the nieces and nephews knowing that their aunt is a stodgy "fuddy-duddy." I don't think it mattered to my grandmother either.

Maybe there is an "s f-d" gene in the family. I want to take a peek in my nieces' and nephews' pantries in a few years.

I'll bet I find a few wooden clothespins.

I THINK IT'S TIME TO CHANGE
HAIRDRESSERS!

Hey, Wait a Minute!

My hairdresser just suggested we "add a little color" to my hair and cheeks!

That's exactly what she said, but what I heard was "Hey granny, you've become old and pale and gray and if we don't do something fast you're gonna be mistaken for a wrinkled albino alligator." The alligator part was because in a previous conversation, she said that I must moisturize my skin more.

Why am I paying this lady - for abuse? I have a mirror. I can see what the aging process is doing, and it's not a pretty sight. I think my many liver spots add a lot of color to my skin!

As we age, many things are taken away from us, like our hearing, sight, flexibility, muscles, skin elasticity, and driving skills, but we are also given some things the young don't have. Things like wisdom, experience, patience, a paid off mortgage, and liver spots!

My hands look like a Dalmatian, but I'm proud of those liver spots. I may as well be because I've tried every bleaching cream on the market and those little darlings are mine to keep.

As for my hairdresser, I've also found a solution for her - change hairdressers.

Keep changing until you find one that is either too shy to tell you about your hair color, dry skin, and ghostly cheeks - or one that is your age and wouldn't dare say anything.

Hey, Wait a Minute!

When did my Christmas desires change from diamond jewelry to a twice-a-month housekeeper?

You can refer to the page in this book titled "Rusty and Dusty," and have a partial answer to this question.

The complete answer lies in the fact that putting diamonds on my hand is like trying to "make a silk purse" - well you know the rest.

Liver spots, wrinkles and diamonds. What's wrong with this picture? I have them all, but I don't put the poor diamonds through the torture of being shown in that showcase.

Diamonds are for young smooth hands, necks and ears in my opinion, and I loved wearing them before I became wise and "mature" - OK past 60. I still love having them and they are laid out in a small row in my jewelry box so I can enjoy them. I can't seem to part with them, or pass them on, even though my nieces' hands, necks and ears are smooth and young - and liver spotless.

My husband spoiled me for years at Christmastime with diamond jewelry and I treasure each gift.

But, this year, for my special present I have my eye on a twice-a-month housekeeper. A housekeeper does not require that my hands, neck, and ears be smooth and free of liver spots, and is a gift that keeps on giving.

Not only will I have a clean house, at least once every two weeks, but I will also have plenty of time to gaze at my diamonds, or just be lazy.

Now there's a Christmas gift.

PRETTY SOON, I THINK I'LL TRY
TO USE THAT LITTLE MOUSE.
IT'S CUTE!

Hey, Wait a Minute!

My computer has taught me the meaning of a "love - hate" relationship.

Actress Angela Lansbury candidly says, when discussing her Internet and computer use, that she's "not very sophisticated," and that she just "keeps punching keys and hopes something comes up."

I've never felt so close to anyone! We've bonded but never met! I think that is the way anyone over the age of 60 learns (I use the term loosely) computers. We are like youngsters trying to learn the piano. Banging away at the keyboard produces terrible results usually, but every now and then we strike a harmonious chord, and that's what makes us keep trying.

My husband calls it "dinking." It's a form of practice. You just keep "dinking" away at the keyboard and remembering which keys you pushed and after 10 or 15 years you'll be a little more comfortable doing it. After all, "dinking" makes perfect.

I was "dinking" away at my keyboard today, and my computer decided that it had had enough of my incessant ignorance and flashed me a "fatal error" message on the monitor. I don't know what "fatal" means to you, but to me, it means it's over - gone - dead - no more.

So I went shopping for another computer.

The salesman assured me that the computer had not died, and there was every possibility that turning it off and back on again could resuscitate it. I did this and my computer is ready for more "dinking." I shall never believe it again. It's just trying to scare me.

Pretty soon, I think I'm going to try out the little mouse that came with it! It's cute!

Hey, Wait a Minute!

I have a library of 150 cookbooks and can never think of anything to have for dinner.

That's not entirely true. I can always think of one thing that I would like to have for dinner, and that's a reservation at any restaurant.

Cooking was a passion for me when I was younger. My dinner parties were always great. I would do all the cooking and preparation for them.

Over the years, my enthusiasm has waned. I still love to have dinner parties but the word "caterer" has entered my vocabulary. Also, party trays from the grocery store have become beautiful to me. I am not above taking my serving dishes to the grocery store and saying "Fill 'em up, I'll be back at 5."

I still enjoy cooking for special occasions - Thanksgiving and Christmas - but the day-to-day meals are suffering from my lack of enthusiasm and imagination. I find myself buying what is easy to prepare instead of what might taste good.

Six months ago, after viewing an infomercial selling a new kind of cookware, I decided my kitchen and I both needed a lift. This would certainly help with my lack of cooking enthusiasm. So, I bought the cookware, and even updated my 25-year-old stove to a new black glass-top range.

That helped the kitchen tremendously.

It did nothing for my daily meal preparation.

The new black glass-top range does, however, make a beautiful background on which to set a silver tray of hors d'oeuvres - just as soon as the caterer arrives to place it there.

Let's party!

Hey, Wait a Minute!

Those infomercials never said
I had to use the exercise equipment -
just buy it!

Five minutes a day - just five minutes a day on this contraption and I'll look like Suzanne Summers!

It looked so easy. All you had to do was get on your knees and roll this wheeled contraption back and forth for 5 minutes once a day, and you'd look like Suzanne. I can hardly wait for it to be delivered.

I paid the shipping and handling (enough that I thought it should be delivered tomorrow) but they promised me that I would have my exerciser in 6 to 8 weeks. That would give me plenty of time to "pig out" and watch TV so that I could really give this equipment a challenge. After all, I couldn't exercise until the equipment arrived.

I was in the middle of a "Golden Girls" rerun the day I heard the UPS horn outside signifying that I had a package. It was here!

As I unwrapped the package I was thinking that I had better get a lighter shade of blond for my hair, as I was definitely a little darker than Suzanne, and short shorts even crossed my mind. However I would probably have time to shop before the transformation occurred.

There it was - in the middle of the den floor. I attached the rollers and got on my knees and rolled - and rolled - and rolled - and rolled - and only 2 minutes had passed.

That's when I decided that I didn't want my transformation into Suzanne to occur too rapidly. All my friends would be jealous.

Besides, "Designing Women" was about to start on channel 40.

Hey, Wait a Minute!

The ticket seller at the movie box office gave me the senior discount without asking me to prove my age!

Years ago, when I was 29, a well-meaning teen-ager called me "Mam."

How depressing that was!

"Mam" is a southern term of respect used for middle-aged to elderly women, and taught to every southern child by every southern Mama. My Mama taught me and I probably depressed hundreds of women with that same "term of respect" throughout my teen-age years.

This teenager, in one respectful word had placed me in that passage from girlhood to womanhood in one second.

I hated it!

I solved the depression problem by running to the nearest department store and buying a leather mini skirt and a too tight sweater. No doubt about it, the new outfit made me look, well, like a "Mam" in a mini skirt and a too-tight sweater.

This passage of time thing is for the birds. The one thing I found out was that you can't go back. Once you've been called "Mam," the passage has occurred. The bell cannot be un-rung.

As for the ticket seller at the movie, I prefer to think that he just glanced at my husband who purchased the tickets and assumed that he was a senior, therefore, his wife must be a senior.

He thought he was doing the purchaser a favor by charging him less. What a sweet guy!

That's my story and I'm sticking to it!

I plan to go shopping after the movie. Maybe I'll have a makeover and a new hairstyle.

I wonder if they sell leather mini skirts in "women's sizes."

Hey, Wait a Minute!

Why do they call it the middle age spread? I've looked like this since I was 30!

I have found the greatest diet ever created! Their nametags say they are Karlee and Kevin, and they work at the local fast food hamburger palace in my hometown.

When I crave a wonderfully greasy cheeseburger piled high with onions, tomatoes, and lettuce with a slab of mayo, some mustard and ketchup with a heaping side of fries, I make sure I go to this palace.

This is because Karlee is the server and Kevin is the cook.

These two must have worked in a piercing parlor before changing careers, because everywhere that can be pierced - they are pierced.

The tongue is the diet watcher for me. Both have little gold studs - 2 or 3 of them - at the edge of their respective tongues. It gives them a lisp when they speak, and no matter how hard I try, I cannot stop staring at those little gold studs.

After hearing Karlee repeat my order to me, my appetite diminishes dramatically. I think the current count is 11 cheeseburgers I have discarded in the "Thank You" garbage receptacle that is placed by the door.

To be effective as a diet, however, I would have to eat here daily - or not eat here daily, so I call this my aid to moderation.

As I said, I have looked like this since I was 30, and have tried many diets with little effect.

I want Karlee and Kevin to know how much I appreciate their work.

They are doing everything they possibly can do to make me skinny.

Hey, Wait a Minute!

I still get "mood swings," and I don't have PMS or raging hormones anymore.

The excuses are gone.

I've nothing to fall back on except "Because I felt like it" as an answer to "Why did you say that to the yard man," or "Why did you yell at the cat?"

I don't think PMS or hormones have anything to do with mood swings. I think that we are all susceptible to crabbiness and/or happiness at any given moment. Stress management gets tougher as you get older, and there are times when you just want to be a spoiled rotten brat. The only salvation is that you are not alone with this feeling.

My sister's answer, when backed into a corner with one of those questions of "Why did you do that?" says simply, "I have absolutely no defense."

What a great line! Not only is it probably the truth, but there is no appropriate "come back" by the questioner. And life goes on.

We get happy with an "up" mood swing and feel guilty about the yard man and the cat for a little while.

It was great in my young and middle years to have the crutches of PMS and raging hormones to blame such behavior on, but in reality, it was probably me being a spoiled brat most of the time. I would never have admitted that when I was younger, but now the phrase "crotchety old lady" doesn't bother me.

I wear it like a badge of honor.

I worked for it. I deserve it.

WHO DO I THINK I'M KIDDING?
IT'S BEEN 30 YEARS SINCE
I WANTED TO DANCE ALL NIGHT!

Hey, Wait a Minute!

I don't feel like an old lady. I feel like a "pre-osteoporosis" babe!

I've been popping calcium pills for 10 years, and I still dread my first bone scan. I am sure that my bones will look like rolled-up sponges, and be about as strong as a cheese doodle. So I'm doing everything I can not to face that problem.

I'm putting off the test!

My doctor doesn't think that this is very good preventative medicine, but I adhere to the theory that ignorance is bliss. The sooner I find out about my bones, the sooner that adds a worry to my list of "dangers," and I simply don't have room on that list right now.

Besides, I'm 62 and in three more years, Medicare will pay for the scan! With medical costs zooming, that could be worth waiting for.

The commercials for calcium say that "It's never too late" to start taking their pills, and I hope they are right. If I have sponges and cheese doodles instead of strong bones, maybe the calcium pills have caused them to be a little less spongier or cheese doodlier than they would have been otherwise.

With this line of reasoning going for me, I think I'll wait for Medicare.

Maybe by that time, I'll feel more like having a bone scan and less like dancing all night.

Who do I think I'm kidding? It's been 30 years since I danced all night!

Hey, Wait a Minute!

Why is my skin still "pruney?"
I took that hot bath
before 9 o'clock last night.

Let's face it, it's "Basset Hound" time for some of us. Our skin just gets too big for our bodies.

I'm sure it has something to do with exercise and muscle tone and proper diet, but frankly, I think some of our skin simply "forgets" as it ages. That makes sense to me because other parts of our body "forget" also. (You can fill in your own forgetful body part here).

Thinking this way gives me an out for not having exercised, and for not having eaten properly.

The people who say, "There is nothing more beautiful and impressive than a wrinkled face" usually do not have wrinkled faces. These people say that each line tells a different story or experience.

What a bunch of bosh!

The only story my lines tell is one of not moisturizing properly, and sunbathing too frequently.

My loose skin gives me a reason not to diet though. With every pound lost, my skin would get bigger, and saggier.

I don't mind being compared to a Basset Hound because they're cute and cuddly.

If there is enough incentive, I'll even fetch your slippers.

I DON'T WANT THE WRONG FINGER
TO FLY UP AT THE WRONG TIME
WHEN I'M DRIVING.

Hey, Wait a Minute!

I found out the best cure for road rage is road resistance! I just don't go anywhere!

During the past few years, road rage has turned deadly, and because of this I feel that I should wear mittens when I drive. I don't want to give the wrong impression by having the wrong finger fly up at the wrong time.

As I live in Florida, it's probably a style "faux pas" but if it saves a life - namely mine - this little kitten will find her mittens.

I am not a hothead, and my fingers usually stay folded around my steering wheel, but with the thousands of automobiles on any expressway today, all vying for the honor of being the lead car, tempers are bound to flare.

I've found a cure for all of this road rage.

I stay at home - or within my little community of about 4 square miles. It has everything I could possibly require to live a full and exciting life.

If I should ever get the urge to vacation or visit family or friends who live far away, I drive on the back roads. The scenery is better and the drivers nicer. They don't seem to be in such a hurry.

I made my "stay at home" decision the same time the State made their decision to add more lanes to the Interstate that leads to Disney World.

When I use that road, I make sure my mittens are handy.

Hey, Wait a Minute!

"Rusty and Dusty" may sound like country singers but in reality, that's a description of most of the stuff in my Florida house.

When there is a combination of high humidity, acid rain, wind, baking sunlight, and laziness, you will have rust and dust!

I have not only described Florida's weather, but the attitude of one of its residents when it comes to cleaning rust and dust - me. I think rust protects the metal and dust protects the furniture, so if ever I feel the need, I'll get some sandpaper for the rust and an ice scraper for the dust, and have my house standing tall in no time.

Just be sure to call before you come - several hours.

I have found that in Florida, one can clean daily, weekly, monthly, or yearly. There's no difference because the day after one cleans, it looks the same as before. I prepare for guests hours before they arrive, not days before they arrive. My "Martha Stewart Image" is in real danger.

I really don't mind the rust and dust because for those two shortcomings, Florida repays its residents with beautiful weather year round, wonderful beaches, and the world's most fantastic flora and fauna. These are the things one learns to appreciate, and to heck with the rust and dust.

Life is slower here.

As for the laziness reference, I prefer to consider myself a "real laid back" Martha.

Hey, Wait a Minute!

When did "bird-watching" become my favorite sport?

There are two types of people who are sport bird-watchers. There are those who tromp through the woods and climb mountains just to catch a glimpse of a yellow-bellied sapsucker, and there are those of us who watch our backyard birdfeeders. Why should I go to them when eventually, they will come to me? I offer food, water, and a bath and don't even charge rent. I prefer to think the birds that come to my backyard feeder are a little smarter than those who do not.

These birds can spot a good thing when they see it.

My lounge chair my bird book and I have spent many happy hours beneath my bird feeders, and I have spotted some very unusual birds that I record in my bird-spotting diary. I use the term "unusual" to describe their personalities, not their pedigree.

There is a "married" couple - Cardinals - who sit and scream at each other on the ground and then one or the other will go to the feeder and eat. I think they are trying to decide who will eat first, or maybe the are shouting a bird blessing for the food which they are about to partake. I've named them "Bonnie and Clyde" because they seem to be "stealing" the food from each other.

Then there is a female Blue Jay who should be wearing a tee shirt that says "Get out of my way, I'm hungry" because she screams the other birds out of the feeder and enjoys her fill. Her name is "Big Mama." Her "husband" joins her quite often and he is dubbed "Big Daddy."

These birds were smart enough to find my birdfeeder and not mind if I intrude on their daily routine family life. That makes me feel wanted and loved.

Funny how "Big Mama" and "Bonnie" seem to scream louder than "Clyde" and "Big Daddy!"

Hey, Wait a Minute!

CHAPTER 5

World at Large

I DECIDED TO BE KIND TO MY NEXT
TELEMARKETER. I ASKED IF HE AND
HIS FAMILY WERE ENJOYING THE
HOLIDAYS!

Hey, Wait a Minute!

Have you hugged your Tele-marketer today?
They call only because they're lonely.

We've given them a bad rap.

In this day of "press 1 if," and "press 2 if" and "press 47 if " telephone computers, one rarely gets to speak to a human being. Home answering machines add to the paranoia suffered by callers.

If your career is tele-marketing, that can get frustrating.

Why do they call at dinnertime? That gives them an edge of actually having someone answer the phone. In their wildest imagination, I don't think they expect to sell anyone anything. They just want to be loved. After a day of computer and machine talking they are looking for a warm friendly voice saying "Hello."

They do understand that a few seconds is all they will get that is warm and friendly because with their next sentence, which identifies themselves, either the phone disconnects, or the answerer becomes icy. If given a chance, these are very nice people, but with very bad career choices.

So, I decided to be kind and caring to my next Tele-marketer. I listened to him for a few moments and when he finished his pre-written recitation, I asked him about his family, and if they were enjoying the holidays.

Now I know how they feel when someone hangs up on them!

Hey, Wait a Minute!

Fruity? Woody? Muscular tones?
It just tastes like wine to me!

I love wine.

However, my taste buds are so unsophisticated that it's hard for me to tell white from red without looking. I have sniffed, schloshed the wine around in my mouth, closed my eyes as if I were thinking, even rolled my eyes and looked at the ceiling, and I have yet to taste a fruit or a piece of wood in my wine.

At "wine tastings," I have seen oenophiles almost have orgasms over the "bouquet" and "tone" of a mouthful of wine. I don't doubt them, I'm just jealous that I can't smell and taste the same thing.

I would love to be able to educate my palette because frankly, I'd like to share the action. All of them seem so happy with wine in their mouths. It's amazing to me that they can tell the subtle differences.

If it were chocolate they were tasting, I could understand. I can tell the difference in every manufacturer of chocolate, and from what area it originated. There is a definite "bouquet" and "resilience" to chocolate made in the northern areas, and a "creaminess" and "liquidity" to the southern chocolates. If you roll them around in your mouth before chewing, you can definitely taste the subtleties. Close your eyes and roll them back as if you are thinking, and the differences are easy to recognize.

I just don't think I will ever understand those "wine people!"

Hey, Wait a Minute!

Whatever happened to the 60's, the 70's, the 80's—or even the 90's

I feel this must be written before the present decade is over because one may easily ask, "Whatever happened to the 60's, the 70's, the 80's and even the 90's," but it would seem weird to ask, "Whatever happened to the 00's." So I'm off to finish this before the ten years of the 00's go by. I'm not ready for the zeros.

I think it would be great to have a mixture of the rebelliousness of the "beatniks" of the 60's, the long hair and attitudes of "finding oneself" in the 70's, the "yuppies" of the 80's, and the computer "cybergeeks" of the 90's. Throw into that mixture the "achievers" of the present and you have a well-rounded person who is ready for anything.

You will note that I left the 50's out because I was in grammar and high school during the 50's and don't care to remember anything from that era.

It's funny how life seems to happen in decades rather than years. It takes ten years for anything frivolous or worthwhile to stick. I think decades were given to the seniors because it's easier to remember in ten-year increments. With each birthday, I'm more and more appreciative of decades.

Now if we could just start counting birthdays by decades, I'd only be 6 for 8 more years.

Maybe I'm on to something here!

I THINK THE OLDER I GET THE MORE I
SUBSCRIBE TO THE "STORK" OR
"CABBAGE PATCH" THEORY!

Hey, Wait a Minute!

Why do all the shows on the Animal Channel concentrate on the mating ritual - in glowing detail?

My mother used to say the doggies were just playing - wrestling with each other - and don't you watch. It's not nice to stare. She always said this with a little giggle and made sure our eyes were otherwise engaged momentarily. I grew up before the baby boomers and we were not privy to such information from adults as to how babies were made - only that the stork brought them, or they were found in a cabbage patch. We accepted that just as we accepted Santa Claus.

Reminiscing, I think I knew there was something more to that wrestling match, but I thought it was probably "dirty" and I just didn't want to know. So I grew up to be fat dumb and happy - until the animal channel emerged.

I am an adult, and fully educated on the way critters procreate. I know they all have sex organs, and I'm glad for them. However, I do not wish those organs stretched across my four foot TV screen in living and glowing color. I have been shown everything from a female tse tse fly's little pinhole to a bull rhinoceros's "winkie" that looked a lot like a Buick LaSabre. Then they show how these organs are used to their full potential. Heaven help me! One gets a whole new picture of what it was like on Noah's boat.

I think the older I get the more I subscribe to the "stork" or "cabbage patch" theory.

Hey, Wait a Minute!

I need a new support group called "CA" - Collectors Anonymous!

Anyone who has to dust 137 glass dogs or 97 marble train engines is a sick puppy, and definitely needs a support group.

I don't know how this "I want them all" attitude creeps into my logical mind when I see another marble train engine or little glass dog. I could understand if I just happened to see another one at an antique show or a garage sale, but that is not what occurs. I search them out, everywhere - on the net, in the stores, at auctions, at garage sales. I even make long distance phone calls to my family to see if they will search for me.

I love all my collections - all my many, many collections - but as I get older, I think I'm turning a corner. Frankly, I get annoyed that those 137 glass dogs and 97 marble train engines require so much of my time and attention to wash and dust.

I've retired and it's about time they did the same.

I keep trying to plant the idea of collecting in my nieces and nephews. I tell them how much fun it is and how much satisfaction and joy they will have, and how beautiful a collection is to display.

So far, I haven't found much interest shown for the glass dogs or the marble train engines, but Christmas is coming.

I miss them already!

Hey, Wait a Minute!

Can you still go through the "less than 10 items" express line at the grocery store with two 6 packs?

Ok, I want a bill presented and laws passed about the express lines at grocery stores!

When I line up at the express lane I want to know the score. I am tired of the "eye daggers" being thrown my way to make me feel guilty about wanting to hurry. Just because I had the foresight to secure a rolling cart to place my 10 items in is no reason for the lady who is holding two babies and 11 items in her arms to be angry at me for planning ahead.

If the grocery stores are going to have these lanes, they need to enforce them.

They could charge you for every item over the ten "maximum limit" and you wouldn't get to take those items home. It would be the amount of your fine. The more items over ten - the bigger the fine. I'm talking enforcement here!

I usually don't bother with the express lines, even though most times I have less than ten items. We eat in restaurants most nights, and our grocery needs are few.

So I just pull up behind the person with half the store in her cart and a stack of coupons an inch thick and enjoy reading the magazines until her check has been approved. In our busy world it's tough to find the time to read, and I feel this is a solution to that problem for me.

The one little hitch with this is trying to get my ice cream to stay ice cream and not a milky puddle on the grocery store floor.

When this happens, the cashier tells me that I should have gone to the express lane.

After all, I only had ten items.

Hey, Wait a Minute!

There should be a mandatory one-night jail sentence for each day a "Garage Sale" sign is left up after the sale is over.

Everyone who is planning a garage sale should accept a "code of respectability" much like the old "code of the West." This code should forbid garage sale signs to be left up after the sale is over.

I don't know how to calculate it, but I have many extra miles on my van from chasing wild-goose garage sale signs. Not only does this include signs left up after the sale is over, but signs having the wrong directions on them.

We garage sale maniacs simply do not have the time to waste hunting sales that do not exist, nor to try and find a misdirected sale.

I speak for all of us as the self-appointed head maniac.

Fortune awaits! You could make us miss the item at the next sale that could be featured on the "Antiques Roadshow!"

It also makes us mad as wet hens!

I'm sure that you or your loved ones would not want to share a roadway with a bunch of stressed out "wet hens" making mid-block U-turns in vans searching for garage sales.

So, if you left a garage sale sign posted from a week ago, get your kids off the street, cause we're coming for you.

We can give the dirtiest looks on the planet, usually followed by a wagging index finger - and you never want that index finger wagged at you.

It's the guilt finger.

Hey, Wait a Minute!

I think my odds of winning the lottery are 50 - 50. They'll either call my numbers, or they won't!

I hate it when newspapers state that your odds of winning the Florida lottery are fourteen million to one, and that you are more likely to be struck by lightning than win the lottery. Are they trying to get people NOT to buy tickets?

Everyone I know dreams of winning the lottery. Plans are even made of how to spend the money. I always think of how I could help mankind or animals, thinking that if I'm altruistic it will improve my chances with the great lottery god of "you win."

I must admit that secretly I see a new house, a trip around the world, and a couple of Porsches in the driveway, but those are just fantasies.

Reports are that most of the winners are unhappy or broke after four years and wish they had never won.

I would like to break that chain.

If I did win, I can promise you that I would never wish that I had not won. I can also promise that I would not be unhappy that I had won. Money doesn't make you happy or unhappy. It's the way you spend it. Maybe it's a test of character to win the lottery by whoever keeps score on our "permanent record."

If that "tester of character" is listening, I'd like to try for an A+. Just so you'll know, my numbers are 2-10-27-34-41-48.

I promise that mankind and animals will come first!

Hey, Wait a Minute!

I only wanted to watch the movie - not rent the theater!

I don't know what young married people do for entertainment today, but when we were first married, there were a whole lot of movies involved. That was because a Friday night on the town meant a movie and a pizza parlor, and if you tried real hard you could keep the total evenings expenses to under six bucks.

I know times have changed and I would be chastised for living in the past by anyone under 30, but we enjoyed our Friday nights out thirty-five years ago and we still do.

Today's young married couples usually have several jobs between the two of them, which is the only way that they can afford to live a cosmopolitan life with money left over for a movie night out.

Expectations of entertainment have become so advanced and sophisticated in our society that the cost of making a movie has become astronomical. Consequently, the ticket prices have become astronomical. Smashing 50 or 60 cars per chase scene, plus paying some movie star 11 million dollars to do the destruction is asinine to me, and I think it makes me angry that they make it look like such fun, but that's another story. I understand why the ticket prices have increased, I just don't agree with it.

We have discovered the 5:00 p.m. "twilight matinee" at the theaters to be wonderful. The tickets, with our senior discount, cost half as much and there are very few people in the auditorium.

If you really hustle, that leaves time for the pizza parlor before you get home for the 9:00 p.m. news.

Jeez! How old am I?

Hey, Wait a Minute!

Why do rainy days receive such bad "press" from all the TV weather reporters?

I happen to prefer rainy days to sunshiny days. There, I've said it, and I probably will have to relinquish my Florida citizenship, or get tarred and feathered and run out of the State.

The "Sunshine State" is a wonderful place to live and the advertisements never mention that we also have rain now and then. I know that people who live in seasonal climates don't understand when I complain about another day of sunshine, but I have even stooped to turning on the sprinkler so the water hits the window, and closing the curtains to make it darker. I close my eyes and dream of inclement weather.

We have been brainwashed to think that sunshine is good and rain is miserable. The press controls our thoughts on this issue as much as they do on presidential elections. Well, I campaign for clouds and rain!

I haven't frolicked in years, but if I ever did frolic again, I'd want to do it in the rain. I love to walk in the rain, sleep in the rain, swim and picnic in the rain, hear the rain on my roof and feel it on my face. The only time I don't like the rain is when it has wind and lightning with it, and the press gives it a name - like "Andrew."

Then, I can't wait to see a little sunshine peek through.

Hey, Wait a Minute!

My newspaper made a mistake - said that Raquel Welch was 60!

Raquel, say it isn't so!

It MUST be a mistake.

Raquel, you will always remain age 25 in my opinion, and I must say you still look closer to age 25 than 60.

Marilyn Monroe would be over 70 now! Oh No!

I remember both of these beautiful ladies from my youth as being the sexiest women in the world. I felt pretty sexy myself then and I think it was partly because of them. We all copied their looks and makeup, and to be honest, even stuffed our bras - admit it ladies - you stuffed your bra. This was before "Wonderbras" existed. Kleenex stock was out of sight and I personally think that all the bra-stuffing had a lot to do with that.

I threw my newspaper at the cat, hoping he would hide Raquel's age with his incessant shedding hair, but no such luck. He just ran out the door giving me one of those "you'll be sorry" looks.

Today's teens are much more honest about such things as bra stuffing, and waist cinching, and that's a good thing. They don't experience the "What happened?" look from the salesperson when they are trying a new swimsuit. It's just not as important to be 36-24-36 anymore.

They have brought an acceptance to their bodies as they are, and don't apologize for them as we did.

That's healthy.

Even Barbie became thicker in the middle, and it's about time, Barbie! You're over 40 now - just like Raquel and Marilyn.

THE DIFFERENCE BETWEEN A
FRESH SALAD AND THE "PRE-TORN,
PRE-BAGGED" ONE IS ASTOUNDING!

Hey, Wait a Minute!

That restaurant is charging me $2.95 for a dinner salad they poured out of a plastic bag!

I love convenience!

I rely on time savers, appliances and cooking tools most of our mothers sadly did not have. However, when I dine in a nice slightly up-scale restaurant, I don't care if they have convenience.

I want good food.

Salads have become distressing since the "pre-packed - pre-torn" ones have been offered to restaurateurs as a convenience.

I think the big white lump of lettuce that lived near the core and has turned brown on the edges initiates my gag reflex.. Also, the leaves seem to be folded as if they have been packed in a too-tight suitcase. The plastic bag also contains a few shreds of carrot with something white on them and red cabbage for color - certainly not for taste. This stuff is in every bag of pre-torn salad from every grocery warehouse or grocery store. You must have seen them, or experienced the taste.

The difference between a fresh salad and the "pre-torn, pre-bagged" one is astounding.

I have calculated the profit for these restaurants that want a pre made salad for convenience. The restaurant gets approximately 20 servings per bag. This bag of pre-made salad costs $1.99 at the warehouse store. At $2.95 per serving, that adds up to $59. Subtract the original cost of $1.99 and that makes a profit of $57.01 per bag.

I think these people are the same ones who sell popcorn at the movies!

Hey, Wait a Minute!

CHAPTER 6

Miscellaneous Madness

Hey, Wait a Minute!

My cat, "Spunky" thinks his name is "Spunkydammit!"

There is some strange little "quirk" given to every cat in the world - and I hesitate to say God-given.

My sister and brother-in-law, who live in Atlanta, have a beautiful silver gray Korat who wants nothing more out of life than to sit on a pile of pillows - between the two of them. "Madame" becomes quite agitated when one of them is not in the room, and trots back and forth to each "meowing" her little head off until her family is one once more.

My husband and I have owned a cat that loved tomatoes. Her name was "Bardmoor," and she preferred tomatoes to fish, shrimp, or meat. "Caldonia," who is allowing us to live with her now must have iced tea. I make 3 or 4 cups each day just to satisfy her habit.

Then there is "Spunky," who received several genes of "stubborn" from whatever genepool made him a cat.

We scream our heads off trying to get him to do something - or not to do something, but until we say "Spunky dammit" he doesn't move.

The tone of voice is inconsequential - from soft and sweet to shouting. The cat still requires "Spunky dammit" for attention of any kind from him. Upon our call he may lift one eyelid, turn his head, or run to us, depending on his mood.

I think he believes his name to be "Spunkydammit," but I also think I detect a little gleam of satisfaction in his eyes each time he hears us call him that.

We're calling him on his terms, and that is what any self-respecting cat demands.

Hey, Wait a Minute!

I just saved 38 cents on a "name brand" toothbrush - but I had to buy a case of 72!

I love to shop in Sam's Club and Costco and can spend hours walking down every aisle and looking at the bargains.

My pantry, freezer, garage, closets, storage shed, rented mini warehouse, and underneath my three beds has never been so well stocked with essentials.

It gives one pause for reflection of the past when we might have had to run to the store for a loaf of bread. Now, we look in our freezer and select the top loaf of the dozen we purchased three months ago at Sam's.

When confronted with so much, my logic gets clouded.

This brings us to the case of 72 "name brand" toothbrushes. They were so beautifully packaged and I thought what a wonderful hostess I would be if a guest forgot his toothbrush. I would, however, need to be running a hotel to use all of the toothbrushes.

Maybe I could give them as Christmas presents! But, I can't remember anyone getting excited on Christmas morning opening a toothbrush.

Rationalization reminded me of how perfect they are for cleaning the grout between the tiles in the bathroom!

Okay, it's time for my good sense and logic to kick in - and it did.

I walked away from the toothbrushes - about three steps before I turned on my heels and went back.

Into my shopping cart they went!

I simply could not pass up a savings of 38 cents on a toothbrush!

Hey, Wait a Minute!

I wash our clothes once a month - just like clockwork!

We each own 31 pairs of underwear.

My husband owns 31 golf shirts, and I own 31 washable blouses. We only own 16 pairs of shorts because I have decided we can wear shorts at least 2 days. I love this casual Florida living!

Everything else goes to the professional laundry or drycleaner.

On the 32nd day I must wash our clothes!

My last washing machine and dryer lasted 35 years. They were both super capacity, and because of that fact, I only required 4 loads per month from each of those units - 2 loads with bleach and 2 loads without bleach - for 35 years. That's only 1680 cycles for each of the units.

No wonder they lasted 35 years!

If you can't guess by now, washing clothes is the domestic chore I hate most, so I have fine-tuned it to a once a month despicable, boring, job.

It's not putting the clothes into the washer that I dislike.

It's taking them out of the dryer.

Folding clothes requires me to spend more time than I want to spend with our wearing apparel.

I know how lucky I am to be able to own a washer and dryer, and what a spoiled brat I am not to enjoy using them.

I'm just glad I wasn't born when the first washer was a river, and a rock, and the first dryer a rope.

Hey, Wait a Minute!

That's my CAT that's in the hospital - not my husband!

Has anyone else noticed the rise in medical care costs for our furry and feathered pets. We love them very much and agree that they should have the same care afforded them as we have.

I can remember taking my cat to the Vet and getting him immunized every year and having to break a "twenty" to pay the bill. Now when I take my three cats in to have their shots, the only thing I break is my bank account. A badly functioning urinary track can cost as much as $300.

Hey, wait a minute, I think Aetna or Blue Cross should provide "furry, and feathered HMO's" Probably, they would be more profitable than regular HMO's, and the patients will be easier to deal with since they find it hard to make phone calls.

The title of this page is precisely what I said when I picked up my sweet little 20 lb. "Bardmoor" cat from a week's stay in a local animal hospital.

I think I've got a solution.

I plan to look for suitable jobs (maybe a sleep study) for the three of them, and let them pay into FICA for a few years. Since 7 cat years are equal to 1 human year, in 9.2 years they will be age 65 and entitled to Medicare.

Maybe then we can think about them eating the tiny cans of fancy food instead of the large cans of the "store brand" stuff.

I Like Ike

BEING BORN AND RAISED IN SOUTH
GEORGIA MEANT YOU WERE A
DEMOCRAT FROM BIRTH TO DEATH.

Hey, Wait a Minute!

Why is my first car considered a "classic" - or worse - an antique?

There it was - a 1960 Ford Falcon.

It was white with a sky blue interior. Both of its bench seats were covered with the same sky blue slick vinyl, with rougher vinyl "insets" in a tasteful pattern. I was sure my parents had paid extra for the insets. It was a gift from my parents to provide transportation for completing my college education.

I put an "I like Ike" bumper sticker on its bumper that almost made my dad reclaim the car. A Republican in the Deep South was, among other things, a traitor. Being born and raised in South Georgia meant you were a Democrat from birth to death.

I now regret putting the bumper sticker on the car, not because I've turned Democrat, but because it caused my dad so much grief.

At a classic car auction that I watched on TV this week, there was a 1960 Ford Falcon being auctioned. The auctioneer was telling the bidders what a "classic" it was, and then the awful word "antique" slipped into his hype. If it were an antique, and I was 21 when it was new, just what does that make me! The car went to the high bidder for about 4 times what my parents paid for mine, and running on it's own was questionable - the auctioneer said so - but they kept bidding. With every bid, I felt older.

Maybe that means, like the car, the older I get, the more valuable I'll become.

Or, maybe it means that running on my own will become questionable.

Either way, I think I'm a "classic" and not an "antique."

Hey, Wait a Minute!

Why do I feel that all the $50,000 surprises on Antiques Roadshow are things I threw away after my Grandmother died?

There is a sign in a local antique store that says, "All prices are increased by 50% if I have to listen to a story about your Grandmother having one of these." The line below it stated that "Prices will be increased by 100% if I must listen to a story about your having thrown one of these in the trash."

It seems we all have the same stories. We want people to be awestruck that we had such a valuable item and casually threw it away.

My husband and I have become devotees of the "Antiques Roadshow" on TV. I am sure that my grandmother had a million dollars worth of china, vases, furniture and rugs in her $14,000 house, because everything I see on the show I remember throwing away when we were clearing out her house.

Of course that isn't true, but one's mind bends truth when memory and money are involved.

Maybe it's wishful thinking, or maybe it makes us feel better to impress whoever will listen. Or - maybe it just dreaming about what could be. Whatever it is, it's fun to watch and recognize items that you actually have seen before.

The most fun is watching the reactions of the owners of the antiques. I've yet to hear one say that they already knew what the item was worth. They are always astonished to hear good numbers and doubtful of the appraiser when they hear bad ones.

As for my Grandmother, memories of her are better than money or antiques - some I treasure - some I forget. The most precious were her hugs - and they were easily worth more than a $50,000 antique.

Hey, Wait a Minute!

Take a Prozac, or have a pedicure - the choice is yours!

I have "Florida feet."

Those are feet that go barefoot most of the time at the beach and at home, and my feet are ugly because I do that. The two "C's" - corns and calluses - haven't added to their "pristine beauty," so instead of having just ugly feet, I have bumpy ugly feet. To have someone caress them and clean and massage them is a little bit of what I imagine heaven to be. I thank heaven for Pedicurists!

No matter how stressed out I feel, a pedicure revives my sense of balance. Take a holiday, Prozac!

There is a wonderful little "instrument," that magically scrapes off the 2 "C's" and turns one's feet from "ugh - lee" to "let's go home and play footsie" gorgeous! When this instrument is placed in the right hands - someone who knows how to use it - there is a transformation that occurs to most feet that would cause the angels to sing. I don't know the name for this instrument but it should be called the "miracle worker" because the odds are always against it and it always seems to come through.

I practically float out of the shop after the final touch (bright red toenails) but, sadly, start abusing my poor feet once more. I certainly don't want to cover them with shoes - they're so beautiful!

From "Florida feet" to fantastic feet in 30 minutes! I think it's time for a trip to the beach!

HILDA   HAL, JR.   HAL

IF THEIR CHRISTMAS LETTER IS TO BE
BELIEVED, HAL, JR. WILL, ONE DAY,
BE OUR PRESIDENT.
YOU GO, HAL, JR.!

Hey, Wait a Minute!

Why do those painfully long "Christmas letters" from casual acquaintances annoy the hell out of me?

I don't care that Hal, Jr. is off to climb Mt McKinley. I don't even know who Hal, Jr. is.

He is evidently the son of Hal, Sr. whom we met with his charming wife Hilda at a Christmas party 4 years ago. I remember chatting with Hilda about the Christmas rush and how the holidays always seem to creep up on us early, but Hal, Jr. was not mentioned. On reflection, I find this amazing after reading the letter about Hal, Jr's accomplishments.

Inside the greeting card we received from Hal and Hilda was a 3-page letter giving us a calendar of events that occurred in the home of Hal Jr., Hilda, and Hal during the past year.

Hal Jr. must be a wonderful student judging by his report card and I feel that if this letter is to be believed, he will one day be our President. His sports feats were unsurpassed last year with the track and football scholarships offered him to very sought-after colleges. He hasn't chosen which one he will attend yet. I wish Hal, Jr. the very best in all his endeavors, but I don't understand why I need to know about these endeavors.

I love receiving Christmas letters from our close friends and family. It's nice to catch up on all the news of the year and find out what our nieces and nephews and their families have accomplished and what their goals are for the coming year. These letters are precious to me, and I save them.

I also plan to save Hal and Hilda's letter because one day when Hal, Jr. becomes President, it may increase in value.

You go, Hal, Jr.!

Hey, Wait a Minute!

Why do they make comforters smaller than sheets and blankets?

I was looking at the ruffle that I had sewn onto my stark, modern, bold-design comforter, and decided the style differences were just too much to accept. So I ripped it off, and left our king-size bed looking as if it were still unmade. The sheets and blanket are hanging down by 8 inches all around the bottom of the comforter. Even if I tuck the offending tails in all around, the comforter still does not come down far enough to hide the tucks.

One solution would be to push one side of the bed against the wall after making it and bring the comforter way down on the side that shows——but then the stark, modern, bold-design is off-center, which makes it appear as if I bought a "second" at an outlet store. There's no way to make it work.

Attention bed linen designers!

Doesn't it make sense that the top covers (as the name implies) need to — uh - COVER the bottom sheets and blankets to have a pretty made-up bed?

What a concept!

This bothers me a lot - every week or two (or three) - when I decide it's time to make the bed!

Hey, Wait a Minute!

When did my curtains become "window treatments" and my rugs become "floor coverings?"

"Window treatments" is an interior decorator's phrase for "I cost about 500 percent more than curtains," and "floor coverings" is the same phrase, except with rugs.

We just had our house painted inside and out, had new carpet installed and investigated window treatments. After careful investigation, I decided that a staple gun, cornices, and "sale" fabric would give me all the window treatment I could stand, financially and in principle. I found a beautiful fabric, borrowed the staple gun from the painter, and never had to sew a stitch.

That's my kind a' curtains! Excuse me -window treatments. I think my windows felt pretty well treated and they were happy with the fresh fabric.

The carpet I selected covered the floor - hence "floor covering." I saved lots of money and satisfied my principles. What more could one ask?

Well, I never counted on having fun making the window treatments and loving the creativity needed to make them beautiful. I would even like to make "window treatments" a second career. I enjoyed it that much.

I probably wouldn't make very much money though. I don't know that many people who could afford my services. Those services and creativity might cost about 500 percent more than just curtains.

Now I get it!

Hey, Wait a Minute!

Why does the "lead azalea" in my azalea garden always die? Is there too much pressure?

They are lined up like a high school band in ever decreasing numbers until we come to the majorette - the "lead azalea" bush. It is a beautiful pink azalea that has been replaced 4 times. It is now sick and I can see replacement #5 well in view.

My theory is that the pressure of being in front of all those other azaleas is simply too much for any poor bush to handle. I plan to test this theory when I replace the bush by planting a friend, another pink azalea to share the lead. Maybe two majorettes are better than one. At least they can talk things over about the constant pressure always facing the leaders - being seen first - setting the tone for the entire garden - always in front for photographs - having their blooms caressed by human hands - people walking too near - all the normal problems lead azaleas have. They need love and understanding as much as fertilizer and water. There's nothing worse than an angry azalea.

I tend to humanize plants and inanimate objects. I try to get "in tune" with them, so that maybe I can imagine their feelings and attitudes. My husband points out that plants and inanimate objects don't have feelings or attitudes and he's probably right, however, he has an automatic pool cleaner named "Sue" and a car named "Annie."

I've seen the way those azalea blooms look at me as I pass by - they want out of the limelight.

I'll probably replant this "lead azalea" before it dies, and if I do, I think it might be in the trombone section - so it can relax among its friends.

Hey, Wait a Minute!

Gabriel Heater and my Grandfather made quite a pair!

It was a big, booming voice and yet it had a tremulous quality to it that commanded attention. That voice was broadcast over the radio every night. The newscaster's name was Gabriel Heater.

My sister and I hated this voice because it meant that my Grandfather would make us sit still with no talking or playing from the start to the finish of the newscast. When you are in the first decade of your life, news of the day is bor-ring!

I think those 30 minute "sit still no talking" stints helped to create patience and understanding in both my sister and in me that will last us a lifetime. We can thank our Grandfather for that.

When we left the room we would mock Gabriel Heater with an outlandish shouting of "Baaaaaad newwws tonight!" and giggle till we got a rap on the fanny from our nearest parent.

Our Grandfather was blind, and the chair with the radio near enough to tune was where he spent much of his time. He was a great thinker and even invented a board with a metal one-line cutout and a clicking typewriter roller that allowed him to hand-write letters to his sons who were fighting in WW2. So listening to Gabriel and writing letters took up much of his days.

Also, I think shouting at my sister and at me to be still and quiet for 30 minutes during his news broadcast gave him some authority that he needed to have.

We both loved our gruff, old Grandfather - but boy, did we hate the thirty minutes of Gabriel Heater!

Hey, Wait a Minute!

Should I tell Neiman Marcus that their sales would double if they would provide shopping carts?

We waddle!

I'm sure you've noticed us. We are the older ladies who are overweight to varying degrees whose spines are screaming because they were not made to handle the excess weight. Add to that touches of arthritis in the hips knees and ankles and you've got the picture. We are the ones who sleep with a pillow between our legs to reduce the pressure on our joints.

This does not mean that we don't have money that we would like to spend at Neiman Marcus. However, by the time we park at the mall, walk the half mile to get into the store and then the 3 acres of floor space that must be navigated, we're mad as hell at everyone, and are not in any mood to browse - much less shop. The display counters do offer a minimum amount of support if you lean on them just right - but a bare minimum. I almost wiped out the Estee Lauder perfume counter yesterday trying to get to a stool that a lady vacated after her "makeover."

So, we often relegate ourselves to Kmart, Wal-Mart, and Target and accept quality and style in clothing that is not Neiman Marcus - but - they have the shopping carts we love to lean on.

There are thousands of us, Neiman Marcus - take notice - we are not doing Daffy Duck impressions, we're trying to spend our money!

Hey, Wait a Minute!

Everybody knows what a great cook she is. Just don't try any of her recipes!

We all do whatever we need to do to maintain or improve our place in society. If your "thing" is cooking, you need to be the best cook possible within your group of friends. You need for your friends to say, "That is the best casserole - cake - roast - dessert - I have ever, or ever expect to put into my mouth. You are the best cook that has ever been put on this earth!"

Well, that may be a little overboard, but I can promise you that's what the cook hears.

Then a mistake is made. The one who is complimenting the cook makes it.

"May I have your recipe?" asks the admirer of the food.

Oops! That puts the poor cook in a predicament. She wants to be nice, and a good friend, and supply the recipe, however, she also wants to remain the best cook in the group.

So, the cook replies, "I'll type it for you and put it in the mail."

Take it from me—Don't try the recipe!

Dining tables are my "thing." Setting them and making them beautiful is what I do better than anyone in my group.

When asked about my beautiful china, I love to say, "When we were in a small village in France, we found it in the tiniest shop. It was manufactured by the people in that village, and is perhaps the only set that ever was or ever will be available."

I just hope they never shop at Pier 1!

Hey, Wait a Minute!

You can have your linens and silks.
I'm a sucker for seersucker!

I think wedding dresses should be made out of seersucker.

I think every piece of clothing should be made out of seersucker! It's the perfect fabric. The wrinkles are already there, so if you remove it from the dryer after it has been sitting there for three days - who can tell. No one is quite sure if the wrinkles are part of the fabric design, or if the clothing has been ignored in the dryer for three days.

A perfect fabric!

I say keep 'em guessing, and kiss your iron goodbye. I have seersucker curtains in my kitchen and bathrooms, and would have seersucker draperies in my living room if I could get anyone to make them.

I cannot imagine anything better than a seersucker tablecloth. Just rip that "puppy" right off the table, throw it in the washer, pull it out of the dryer (in three days), put a daisy on top of it, and you're ready for drop-in guests! No ironing - no folding. Set that table and yell "Come to dinner!"

I don't know who invented seersucker, but I'd like to know, so I could give this person a big fat kiss.

I know that it is a very "casual" fabric and that there are those of you who wouldn't be "caught dead" in it, but I'd be willing to bet that you aren't a senior citizen who lives in Florida.

We've smartened up!

HE MAY WEAR SIZE 32 JEANS, BUT HIS
WAIST IS SIZE 44!

Hey, Wait a Minute!

My neighbor brags that he wears size 32 jeans just like in college, and he does - but his waist is size 44!

He just pulls the jeans up as far as they will go, which is about 4 inches past where his hips bend, tucks in his flannel shirt, buttons up, and quickly gets a belt drawn around them tightly to hide his "fruit of the looms."

There is about a 50 - 50 chance that these critters will stay up.

The crotch of the jeans hangs about mid-thigh, and it takes three, 2-inch rolls to keep the pant's legs from dragging the ground. The belt of choice is a black number with a big metal buckle that always seems to be looking at the ground in agony.

There are many men who dress like this. I don't know if they think that everyone is allowed only one size from puberty to death, or if they don't like to shop for clothes.

Either way, my heart goes out to this neighbor every morning when I see him leave for work. He has a look that is somewhere between pain and terror on his face. Pain because that belt is squeezing his thighs and terror that his jeans are going to drop right on the ground and expose those "fruit of the looms."

I offered my neighbor some of my husbands jeans that were new, but too small for him, but he politely turned me down saying, "Thanks anyway, but they are way too big for me. I wear size 32 - just like in college."

I think my neighbor is trying to make a fashion statement and is willing to suffer for it.

That metal belt buckle must pinch his "periwinkle" every time he sits down!

Hey, Wait a Minute!

Why do I have 400 pictures of my cat?

At most - I mean allowing for extra development (so to speak) you need - maybe - 4 photos of your cat. One at babyhood, when it's cute and cuddly and playful, one at that awkward teen age spurt of ugly growth (if you must), and maybe two more after it has attained adulthood and full growth. After that—it's the same cat. There are no changes in the way it looks. I have drawers and albums full of photos of my cat - sleeping, running, playing, dozing, eating, drinking, smiling, frowning, hissing, and climbing.

All cats do these things.

Then, I have photos of my cat on the kitchen counter, on the dining table, clawing at a tennis ball on TV, sitting on a doll's lap, sleeping on my husband's lap, playing with balls on the Christmas tree, drinking from the swimming pool, asleep on the diving board, climbing a tree, chasing a dog, asleep on the roof of our house, and sitting in the window waiting for us to get home - you get the picture (sorry).

All cats do these things also.

These stacks of photographs have caused a minimum outlay of cash that I find hard to comprehend. The film is expensive enough, but the development of the film - especially when you order an extra set to share with anyone who will say "Isn't that cat precious" is astounding.

Add to that the outlay for the beautiful chest of drawers I purchased only for photo storage and you're getting up into the "money for a new compact car" category!

Ordinarily, you would think that an irresponsible thing to do, but you haven't seen my cat.

It's the prettiest cat in the world—and the smartest——and the funniest—and the most photogenic.

Why, it's just precious!

About the Author

Dee Logan fought becoming eligible for Social Security. She lost.

Meanwhile, she was a grammar school teacher, an office manager, and an insurance company statistical analyst. She has also raced and rallyed in sports cars, crewed on several different one-design sailboats, co-chaired a PGA professional golf tournament, and is a nationally accredited Flower Show Judge.

She was born and raised in Cordele, Ga., and attended Young Harris College.

Currently, Dee lives with her husband and two spoiled cats in Central Florida.